THE CELTS

Llyfrgelloedd Caerdydd
www.caerdydd.gov.uk/llyfrgelloedd
Cardiff Libraries
www.cardiff.gov.uk/libraries

John Farrelly was born and raised in a village just outside Newry, Co. Down. He wouldn't say his family home was small but the front and back door was the same. He enjoyed school and thinks the education system in Irelandia is the bestest. After dropping out of art college, he worked in an amusement park. He was fired but he took them for funfair dismissal. Then he became a freelance caricature artist. It's a very secure job – no one else wants it. The O'Brien Press stupidly let him write and illustrate the first book in the **Deadly! Irish History** series about the Vikings and now they can't get rid of him. This is the second book in the series.

THE CELTS

WRITTEN AND ILLUSTRATED BY JOHN FARRELLY

THE O'BRIEN PRESS
DUBLIN

Dedication

For my sisters, Marie, Shelagh and Imelda, who gave me lots of love, encouragement and most importantly, paper.

Acknowledgements

I'd like to thank The O'Brien Press for giving me another chance to make history and Dr Matthew C Stout for his expert advice. Thank you to my nephew Conor Fearon for his Irish language prowess. Also, thanks to the staff at Navan Centre & Fort, Armagh.

First published 2020 by The O'Brien Press Ltd,
12 Terenure Road East, Rathgar, Dublin 6, D06 HD27, Ireland.
Tel: +353 1 4923333; Fax: +353 1 4922777
E-mail: books@obrien.ie
Website: www.obrien.ie
The O'Brien Press is a member of Publishing Ireland.

ISBN: 978-1-78849-130-3

Copyright for text and illustrations © John Farrelly
Design: Bex Sheridan
Copyright for typesetting, layout, editing, design
© The O'Brien Press Ltd

1 3 5 7 6 4 2
20 22 24 23 21

Printed and bound by Norhaven Paperback A/S, Denmark.
The paper in this book is produced using pulp from managed forests

Published in

DUBLIN
UNESCO
City of Literature

Contents

A SERIOUS NOTE ON WRITING ABOUT THE CELTS

There are really three versions of Celtic history. The first is what archaeologists and historians have unearthed through hard work and research. The second is from what people, like the Greeks and Romans, wrote about them at the time, which is likely to be a bit biased. And the third is the myths and sagas the Celts told around the fires of their roundhouses and which were written down mostly by Christian scribes centuries later. Although these tales are full of larger-than-life characters and fantastic derring-do, they are likely to have been exaggerated over the years and then censored by the monks who wrote them. But we can still discover within them loads of useful information about the Celts and their wonderful, rich, imaginative world. However, no one can be absolutely sure everything said about the Celts is true, and the pages that follow take inspiration from all three sources.

WHO WERE THE CELTS

The word *Celt* comes from the Greek word *Keltoi*, the name the Greeks called a group of people living in Europe nearly three thousand years ago. What Keltoi means we don't know, but the Celts were feared and respected by their enemies. At one time, the Celts were the most powerful people in central Europe and there were loads of Celtic tribes, who spoke a similar language. They spread outwards across Europe, making their way to France, Britain and Ireland. It's not known exactly how and when the Celts came to Ireland, but it is thought they began arriving around 700–600 BCE. Later Celtic settlers brought with them a new metal called iron, which replaced the weaker metal bronze. This is what historians call the Iron Age.

very successful in establishing them-
which they did over a long period of
nce. Some Celtic tribes lived peacefully
tive Irish, while others took what they
. Eventually, they became more or less
one people, and though some historians don't like the
use of the word 'Celtic', it has come to be used in a
general way to describe the people, culture and art in
Ireland from 700 BCE to the arrival of Christianity in
the early 5th century. This book is about that period in
Irish history.

Irish Celts took on a flavour of their own – they were
different in lots of ways from the other Celtic tribes living
in Europe and even across the Irish Sea in Britain. Even
after Saint Patrick arrived on Irish soil, many pagan
Celtic practices stayed the same for centuries, and Ireland
still considers itself a Celtic country.

Come now on a journey to discover what these Celts
were like – what they believed in, how they lived and
died, and whether they were as *DEADLY*! as we have
been told.

CELT MÍLE FÁILTE
THE CELTS COME TO IRELAND

Although people had been living in Ireland for thousands of years – some of the monuments they built may be older than the Egyptian pyramids – the Celts did not start coming to Ireland until around 700 BCE. A book written in the 11th century, called the *Leabhar Gabhála Éireann* (Book of Invasions), describes a series of six violent invasions by Celtic tribes, but historians now believe the Celts arrived gradually – they didn't 'invade'.

Not a lot is known about this period in Ireland's history so it's shrouded in mystery. An ancient Greek historian called Diodorus Siculus said that the Irish ate human flesh. A Roman called Pomponius Mela said that you couldn't grow crops in Ireland, but there was so much grass that cattle would burst open from eating it.

A scholar called Claudius Ptolemy made the first known map of Ireland around the year AD 140. Although it looks like it was drawn by an infant because they didn't have the technology to make accurate maps back then, Ptolemy's map provides lots of useful information about Ireland at the time.

BY PTOLEMY AGE 4

Ptolemy called Ireland *Iwernia*, which is thought to mean 'abundant land', and from which we probably get the Irish names *Ériu* and *Éire*. Not only are there rivers we recognise as the Boyne, Shannon and Liffey, but there are also a few placenames and the names of some of the Celtic tribes who lived on the island. Though these tribe names are written in a mix of Greek, Latin and Arabic, modern scholars think they represent the tribes mentioned in stories.

For instance, the *Voluntii* were also known as the Ulaid, which later became Ulster. The *Dumnonii* are thought to be the Domnainn, who settled in Leinster and later in Connacht. The *Menapii* are reckoned to be the Monaig, who went on to give their name to Fir Manach (Fermanagh).

While the Romans knew Ireland existed, they did not try to invade it the way they did Britain. A Roman general called Agricola, who had already conquered much of Britain, did think about it, but he was recalled to Rome by the emperor. Soon after arriving, he died from something he ate.

Personally, I think the Romans didn't invade because they heard the Irish ate each other and had exploding cows!

The Celts divided Ireland into four provinces, and the point in the centre where the provinces met was named the Hill of Uisneach. This was a very special place as it was the sacred centre of Ireland (sometimes called the navel of Ireland) and supposedly the burial place of two of the most important Celtic gods called Lugh and the Dagda, who we'll meet later.

WE COLLECTED ALL THAT *BELLY BUTTON FLUFF* FROM THE HILL OF UISNEACH!

The Celts were always fighting with each other – like, all the time. Fighting was as natural to the Celts as breathing or eating – it was just something they did. It meant, though, that there could be no real unity in Ireland, and it was one of the reasons why people like the Vikings came along centuries later and were able to establish themselves in Ireland.

The Celts carved out a new province for themselves in the centre of the island, calling it Mide, which means 'middle'. Kings built themselves royal sites in all five provinces: Eamhain Mhacha in Ulster, Cashel in Munster, Dún Ailinne in Leinster, Rathcroghan in Connacht and the Hill of Tara in Meath.

Tara is the best known of the royal sites and was a special place from long before the Celts arrived. Nowadays, it just looks like a big figure of eight on top of a hill, but back in the day it must have looked very impressive. Some of its features certainly have impressive names, such as Mound of the Hostages, the Banquet Hall, Gráinne's Fort and Fort of the Kings. These were all names thought up in the 19th century, though, and scholars can only make educated guesses as to what all these features were used for. Here's what it might have looked like back then:

1. Mound of the Hostages
2. Stone of Destiny
3. The Inauguration Mound (The Forrad)
4. The Banqueting Hall
5. King Cormac's House
6. The Rath of the Kings
7. King Lóegaire's Rath

It's thought The Hill of Tara was used for thousands of years to inaugurate (a fancy word for 'crown') Irish royalty, right up to around AD 500. The *Lia Fáil*, or Stone of Destiny, is a legendary granite stone that stands on a mound called *An Forradh* (The King's Seat). According to the stories, it is supposed to cry out when the rightful ruler of Ireland places his foot upon it.

OWW! AT LEAST TAKE YOUR SHOES OFF FIRST!

According to the *Leabhar Gabhála Éireann*, gods called the *Tuatha Dé Danann* brought the Lia Fáil to Ireland. They also brought other magical items like the *Claíomh Solais* (Sword of Light), the *Sleá Bua* (known in English as the Spear of Lugh, though the word *bua* means victory) and the *Coire Dagdae* (The Dagda's Cauldron).

Historians reckon the Lia Fáil that sits on the Hill of Tara today is not the same one that was there originally. Some people think that the Stone of Scone – a stone chair on which the kings and queens of England and Scotland were crowned – was the original Lia Fáil and was stolen from Tara. Others think the stone is still buried somewhere at Tara, awaiting the time when Ireland needs a High King again. Like a lot of things about the forgotten history of Ireland, we'll probably never know for sure.

As well as bringing iron to Ireland, the Celts introduced another important development. By around 100 BCE, they had built a series of roads called *slite* that stretched outwards from the east coast to Waterford, the Shannon, Galway Bay and Sligo, and northwards to the coast of Co. Antrim. These early motorways were made from felled trees, stones and planks that covered the soft, boggy ground and were wide enough for two chariots to pass one another.

So now we know a bit about who the Irish Celts were, let's find out how they lived their lives.

SETTLE DOWN NOW!
CELTIC SOCIETY

Go and get a dice. I'll wait for you here. Huh? Whaddaya mean, 'It's one *die* and two *dice*?' Er, I knew that, I just wanted to see if you did.

Right. Throw the die. Whatever number you roll, you can find out who YOU could've been if you were born into Celtic society.

You rolled a one – congratulations! You got the head honcho's job – the king! Ireland is made up of loads of tribes ruled over by a king. A tribe is made up of many *finte*, or family groups.

Sometimes, there is even a High King of Ireland or *Ard-Rí na hÉireann*. You can hardly move for kings in Celtic times!

If there is truth in the legends, then sometimes there are queens as well – Queen Macha Mong Ruadh is said to have ruled Eamhain Mhacha near Armagh, and Queen Meadbh (or Maeve) is at the centre of the famous Irish epic, the *Táin Bó Cúailnge* (The Cattle Raid of Cooley), which features Celtic superhero, Cú Chulainn. But men rulers are a lot more common.

You're the king or queen, so what you say, goes. End of. There's a story about a king who made each of his guests eat a mouse and when one of them gagged while putting the tail in his mouth, the king had him killed, saying, 'eating a mouse includes the tail'. YUMMY!

You could become a king – anyone could – so long as your father and grandfather were nobles. The king is always chosen, a bit like how presidents and prime ministers are elected nowadays and not like modern royal families who are just born into it. But being a king isn't all fun and games. If something goes wrong, like a famine or a war, it's likely YOU'll get the blame and will have to face dire consequences.

You rolled a two – that's good. Give yourself a pat on the back because that means you're a noble. You are wealthy and own lots of land, cattle, gold and slaves. Hooray!

All this wealth and status doesn't come free. You still have a job to do. Maybe you're a warrior and will have to fight for the king if another tribe decides to raid your lands. You could be a brehon, a learned person who knows the law and is qualified to judge criminals, or a physician who is skilled in healing. Perhaps you are one of the *Aos Dána* or 'people of the arts': a *file* (poet), a *bard* (musician and storyteller), a *seer* (prophet) or a *druid* (priest or priestess).

If you are a file or bard, it might surprise you that poets and storytellers are thought of so highly in Celtic society, but the fact is, everyone thinks you have supernatural powers! You can compose a poem that praises your king for his bravery and generosity and make his name live forever. Or you can tell a satire about him that makes him look stupid and uncool and make people laugh at him. One file even used a poem to kill!

Before he was murdered, a king's poet called Cúán Úa Lothcháin caused the bodies of his killers to rot away within an hour – while they were still alive! He did this with a poet's spell. So the filí are much feared and respected, a bit like my old maths teacher. I still have nightmares.

Not bad! You rolled a three, which means you're a skilled craftsman. The Celts like to fight and they like to look good doing it, so skilled blacksmiths and craftsmen are highly respected. If you're a blacksmith, you make practical things for people, such as weapons, tools, cooking utensils, chains, horse harnesses, bridles, metal 'tyres' for chariot wheels, and objects like firedogs which are used to hold logs in place in an open fire.

Or perhaps you're a craftworker who uses bronze, silver, gold, glass and enamel to decorate weapons, make brooches, torcs (thick armbands and necklaces), bracelets, earrings, beads, rings, mirrors and statues.

Ah, you've rolled a four. You're ordinary Joe Celt. You work on land you rent from a noble, on which you grow crops and raise animals.

Or perhaps you're a Celtic woman who runs a very busy household. Preparing and cooking food takes up a big part of your day. Your children also help out with chores as there are no schools in Celtic times.

There'll be more on everyday Celts later on.

I WISH THERE *WERE* SCHOOLS SO I DIDN'T HAVE TO DO THESE *STUPID CHORES!*

GRIND! GRIND!

Nyehh. You rolled a five which isn't the best, but it definitely could be worse.

You are a *labourer*. Not quite a slave, but you own hardly anything at all. In fact, by law you're not allowed to own anything. You work the land of a noble who lets you live there and grow food for your family, but you can't leave it without permission. Be prepared for a life of very hard work, producing stuff mostly to give away to someone else, and being told what to do. You cannot vote when it comes to electing a new king, nor do you have the same rights as other members of the tribe.

The good news is that if you work hard enough and please the noble on whose land you work for the next fifteen or twenty years, he may reward you with a wee bit of land of your own. Gee, thanks.

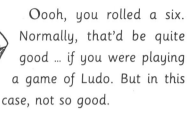

Oooh, you rolled a six. Normally, that'd be quite good ... if you were playing a game of Ludo. But in this case, not so good.

Dirty, stinky, lazy, horrible ... no, I'm not talking about your brother, though he might well be all these things. I don't know him. I'm talking about YOU — a humble slave or *mogh* (bondsman) or *cumhal* (bondswoman).

Not every household has slaves, but the richer ones do. You work for a noble family. You come from another tribe and were captured in a raid. You are given all the really difficult, heavy, dirty, dangerous, smelly work to do. Jobs like ploughing, mining, digging for bog iron, collecting manure, grinding grain, cleaning, tidying and fixing things.

Your back-breaking chores are endless and sometimes you have to wear heavy chains. The best you can hope for is that your master rewards your hard work with freedom and you can become a labourer or you're sold to a nicer noble family, but don't hold your breath. Slaves are considered practically worthless in Celtic society. At least you're in good company – Saint Patrick was a noble boy from Britain who was captured by Irish pirates, sold into slavery to an Irish king and put to work minding sheep on the side of a mountain.

Every person in Celtic Ireland belonged to a family group called a fine, which included parents and their kids, aunts, uncles, cousins and their kids as well as grand parents and great grandparents. If some-one in the group broke the law and was unable to pay com-pensation, the wider family group was responsible for paying it. You could say that it was the fine who had to pay the fine!

This is King Conchúr. You wouldn't call him a liar to his face, but he doesn't always tell the truth. Which of his statements are true, do you think? **Answers below**.

A) IF A KING LOST A LIMB OR AN EYE IN BATTLE, HE WOULD ALSO LOSE HIS POSITION AS KING.

D) A KING CAN KILL ANYONE HE LIKES AND NOTHING WILL HAPPEN TO HIM.

B) A KING DOES NOT LEAD HIS WARRIORS INTO BATTLE.

E) A KING CAN BE KILLED BY HIS TRIBE IF THE CROPS FAIL.

C) WHEN A KING DIES, HIS FIRST-BORN SON BECOMES THE NEW KING.

ANSWERS: Conchúr is king of the liars! He told the truth only twice. a) True. A king had to be physically perfect. b) Heck, no! A king had to lead his men right into the thick of the fighting. c) Nope! When the king snuffed it, there was a scramble to be the next king. d) Nuh-uh. Everyone had an honour-price – a value on their life. The High King of all Ireland could kill the lowliest labourer, and he'd still have to pay a fine, or dire, to the labourer's family. e) True! The king could be sacrificed by his own druids if any natural disaster befell the tribe.

CHE FIANNA

We've seen how Celtic society was made up, but what about the people outside society? I'm talking about Fianna warriors, who are mentioned in many Irish tales.

These were young men, aged around 17–20, who were not yet old enough to inherit land and so wandered the wilderness and survived by hunting, fishing and foraging. They were lawless, rowdy youths who hung around in small groups, causing trouble and hassling passers-by. (Sounds like a Friday night where I live!)

Some fianna earned a living as mercenaries – paid soldiers – when tribes fought with each other, which was often. Others became *díbheargaigh* or bandits and robbed people.

But the fianna weren't always bad. They did have a code of conduct they tried to live by. Amongst other things, *Tales of the Ossian Cycle* advises them:

Utter not swaggering speech, nor say thou wilt not yield what is right; it is a shameful thing to speak too stiffly unless that it be feasible to carry out thy words.

In other words, don't be a smarty pants.

Two-thirds of thy gentleness be shown to women and to those that creep on the floor (little children) and to poets, and be not violent to the common people.

Be kind to ladies, kids, poets (eh?) and ordinary folk.

The legendary Fionn Mac Cumhaill was the leader of a band of fianna warriors. More on him later.

ALL ROUND THE HOUSES
WHERE THE CELTS LIVED

Most of us live in cities, towns and villages nowadays, in strong brick houses with walls and fences and locks on the doors. The most dangerous animal we can expect to come calling is next door's tabby cat pretending her owners haven't fed her. The Celts lived in a land that was covered mostly in thick forests – they had no cities or towns – and in those forests were all kinds of dangerous creatures, like grey wolves, wild cats and wild pigs.

Also, the Celts lived in a time when rival tribes would have had eyes on each other's cattle, treasure and slaves and could launch a raid at any given moment.

With all that in mind, where would YOU choose a spot to build your house?

a) Slap, bang in the middle of the forest.
b) In a big, wide open space.
c) On top of a hill.
d) In the middle of a lake or river.
e) On the edge of a cliff.

If you chose a), congratulations – a neighbouring tribe has just ambushed you, robbed all your stuff and you've become dinner for a family of wolves!

If you chose b) or c) you are quite right. This is exactly where the majority of Celts decided to build their homes. Most tribes lived in scattered farming communities near a water and timber supply and watched out for each other. People believed for years that the Celts lived in ringforts or raths, where they encircled themselves with a ditch and wooden fencing to keep out wild animals and intruders, but historians now know these were not built until the much later Christian times. Kings and their families probably lived in some kind of fort or stronghold but ordinary Celts lived in buildings called roundhouses.

Some roundhouses were made with large stones held together with clay. The Celts also constructed smaller buildings that they used to shelter animals, prepare food, make leather and store grain. You can see a reconstructed Celtic roundhouse at the Navan Centre in Co. Armagh.

If you chose d), it's not as silly as you might think. Dwellings called crannógs were roundhouses that were built in the middle of a lake, river or bog, where the only way a wolf could get at you was if he knew how to row a boat!

You can see a reconstructed crannóg at the Craggaunowen Project in Co. Clare.

If you chose e), you are also correct. These were called promontory forts and there were over 350 of them perched on cliff edges along the coast of Ireland or on remote mountaintops. Although some date from Christian times, there are others that go back to the Iron Age and even further. It's thought they were built to keep a watchful eye for invaders by sea and by land.

Carved stone or wooden boundary posts marked the edges of each tribe's territory. Cross them and you'd be in serious trouble.

Some of these boundaries still exist today in modern Ireland.

INSIDE A ROUNDHOUSE

No smoke hole. Smoke went out through thatch

Roundhouses lasted about 10 years and were home to about 12-14 people. Smaller animals were taken into the house at night for warmth and protection. Geese acted as guard dogs. They had great eyesight, were very noisy and territorial and couldn't be bribed with meat like dogs could.

Meat and fish hanging in smoke for preservation

Thatch of river reed and hazel

Two woven willow wattle walls with straw filling and the outside covered in daub (mix of mud, straw and dung)

DEADLY MEDLEY!

Can you find these things?

☐ Goat and sheepskins (hint: on floor)

☐ Cauldrons

☐ Fidchell board game

☐ Leather tanning frame

☐ Child minding the fire

☐ Slave gathering dung for manure and daub

☐ Goose guard 'dog'

☐ Animal pens

☐ Oven

☐ Quern (hint: two stones that were used for grinding corn)

☐ Butter churn

Answers on pages 142–3

DEADLY! CRAFTY — A ROUNDHOUSE

1) To make the roof, draw a circle on a piece of thin card. You can use a compass, or if you want a bigger house, use a pencil tied to a piece of string and, with the other end fixed down, draw out a big circle.

2) Draw a line from the middle of the circle to the edge, then draw another one at an angle to the first. The smaller the gap between your two lines, the steeper the roof will be. A right angle or slightly less is best.

3) Cut out the circle and along both lines.

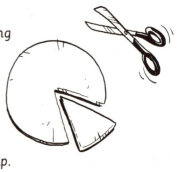

4) Overlap the ends to form a cone. Tape or glue the overlap.

5) To make thatch, glue straw or strips of yellow paper onto the roof. Or just draw it on with a yellow marker.

6) For the walls, measure the diameter of the bottom of the roof and cut a strip of card three times that length. (If the diameter is 15 cm, the strip will need to be 40–45 cm.)

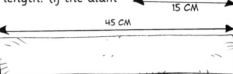

15 CM

45 CM

7) Cut the strip to roughly the same height as your roof. Cut a slot for the door, but don't cut all the way to the top.

8) Paint the card brown and add some lines for a wattle and daub effect. Or paint the card grey and draw on a stone effect. Stick the ends together.

BROWN

9) To make a base, use green card or card painted green. Add some lines for a grass effect, and even some flowers.

WARRIOR BEEN?
WE HAVE WORK TO DO!
CELTIC WAY OF LIFE

We've already seen that the Celts had many different jobs, but the main one was farming. Most freemen farmers worked on land they rented from a noble.

Sowing seeds

Scaring birds away from seed

Weaving cloth

Spinning wool

Weeding and picking stones from soil

This is Farmer 'Fibber' Fintan. He plants seeds of doubt in people's minds sometimes. Which of his statements do you think are true? **Answers below.**

A) CELT FARMERS GROW WHEAT, BARLEY, OATS, CORN, RYE, HAY, CABBAGES, POTATOES, ONIONS, CELERY, PARSNIPS, TURNIPS AND LEEKS.

C) THE CELTIC GOD OF AGRICULTURE IS CALLED THE MORRIGAN.

D) THE MORE CATTLE YOU HAVE IN CELTIC IRELAND, THE MORE POWERFUL YOU ARE.

B) SOME FARMS HAVE BEEHIVES.

ANSWERS: a) All true, except potatoes didn't arrive in Ireland until the 17th century. b) True. Bees were kept in wicker beehives, and their honey was used to sweeten foods and to make mead, a type of wine. c) False. The Dagda was the god of agriculture, fertility, strength, magic and wisdom. The Morrigan was a goddess of war and death. d) True. There were few coins. A person's wealth was measured by how many cows he/she had.

THE CELTIC YEAR

All Celts were close to nature, in that they had to make their own food, clothes and houses using what nature provided. If you had no food, you died! So farming was closely tied in with the Celts' religion. There were four major festivals in the Celtic year.

The Celtic year started around our Halloween time, 31 October, marking the descent into winter, and the Celts called this Samhain. The cattle were brought in from the summer pastures, and food from the harvest was stocked up for the cold months ahead. Meat and fish were salted or smoked to preserve them, and grain was stored in pits to keep it dry. Bonfires were lit and the Celts shared in a feast. After the festival they re-lit the fires in their roundhouses from the sacred bonfire to protect them and to keep them warm during winter.

You have the Celts to thank for coming up with the idea of Halloween, the time of year they believed the veil with the Otherworld was at its thinnest and the spirits of the dead returned to the land of the living. *Wooooooo!*

Imbolc marked the end of winter, around 31 January. The hardest part of the year was over and spring began. Lambs and calves were born, the days lengthened and farmers got ready to get back to work. Imbolc was an important time to predict the weather for the summer.

One Celtic belief was that if the weather was really bad on the day of Imbolc, a great summer was on the way. This was because a pretty horrible weather goddess called the Cailleach would gather firewood only for herself if Imbolc was nice and dry and she would make winter last longer. But if Imbolc was wet and windy, that meant the Cailleach had gone to sleep and winter would soon be over.

Bealtaine was the start of summer, around 1 May. Cattle were driven back out onto their summertime pastures between two bonfires, which was thought to protect the cattle from diseases. Bealtaine was celebrated with lots of singing, dancing and feasting. We still have this festival, now a bank holiday called May Day.

Lughnasa (*Lúnasa*) marked the beginning of the harvest, around 1 August, when the crops that had been growing all summer were taken in. It's named after Lugh, the Celtic God of light and fire. Everyone helped to bring in the harvest and it was another time to celebrate because a good harvest meant you could survive the long, cold, dark months of winter. After they'd offered the first of the harvest's corn to Lugh, they sacrificed a bull which they then feasted on.

Here's a couple of Celtic recipes you might want to try if you're not up for sacrificing a bull.

A DEADLY CELTIC COOKBOOK

CRUBEENS OR PIG'S TROTTERS

This is a rather lovely pork dish the Celts ate, seeing as no part of the pig was wasted … except the *oink!* And it's still popular in parts of Ireland today.

Serves 4–6

4 pig's trotters
1 onion cut into four pieces
1 chopped carrot
2 peeled & halved garlic cloves
1 bay leaf
2 sprigs of thyme
5–6 black peppercorns
Handful of fresh parsley*

Put all the ingredients into a big pot and cover with cold water. You don't need to add salt as the crubeens are already quite salty. Bring to the boil then simmer for 3–4 hours until the meat is falling off the bone. Serve with some boiled cabbage.

Don't worry, this dish is very tasty and won't leave you feeling too *offal.*

* Some of these ingredients may not have been available in Celtic Ireland, but we can cheat a little bit!

CELTIC BREAD

Bread was often made by cooking small, flat pieces of dough on a hot stone or on a flat iron pan heated over a fire.

Serves 3–4

100g butter or lard
250g wholemeal flour
Pinch of salt
1 egg
3–6 tablespoons of milk

Mix the butter or lard into the flour. Add a pinch of salt. Mix the egg and milk and add to make a firm dough. Pinch off small pieces and roll into balls, then flatten with your hands. Put on a hot, greased griddle or frying pan. Cook each side for about 5 minutes.

This tasty bread is perfect for scooping up food instead of using a spoon and for soaking up meat juices or crubeen gravy.

FUN AND GAMES

It wasn't all just about survival in Celtic times – they knew how to have a good time too. Here are a few games and pastimes they had, some of which may seem very familiar ...

FIDCHELL

Fidchell ('wood wisdom') was a board game the Celts played, similar to chess or draughts. It was invented by the god Lugh, and Irish sagas, such as The Táin, talk about gods and kings playing it, and it's likely ordinary Celts played it as well. The modern Irish word for chess, ficheall, comes from it, though the two games are very different. The boards the Celtic kings used must have been big as they're described as being 'heavier than a child could easily carry'. It's said kings had fancy, show-off boards and pieces made from gold, bronze and other precious materials.

The rules weren't written down so historians and games experts have had to make guesses as to how it may have been played. It was like fighting a miniature war, and if there was one thing the Celts loved, it was fighting. A similar game to fidchell was *brandubh* or 'black raven'.

Follow the instructions to make your own (smaller!) board. For the playing pieces, you can use plastic counters from other games you might have around your house.

 FIDCHELL BOARD

1) Cut a square, measuring 33 x 33 cm, out of a thick piece of card.

2) With a ruler, draw a border all the way around, 1.5cm from the edge of the card.

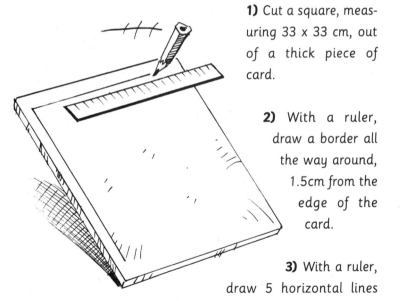

3) With a ruler, draw 5 horizontal lines across the board, spaced 5 cm apart.

4) Draw 5 vertical lines down the board, spaced 5 cm apart.

5) Along the edges of the board and where the lines cross, draw a large dot. You should have 36 squares and 49 dots.

6) Draw a circle around the centre dot. This is the king's 'throne'.

7) You can decorate the edges of your board with a Celtic knot pattern if you like. Trace this one onto tracing paper, turn the tracing paper over and transfer the tracing onto the board. Do this over and over until you reach the edges of the board.

HOW TO PLAY FIDCHELL

You will need:

16 blue playing pieces (the attackers)
8 green playing pieces (the king's defenders)
1 yellow playing piece (the king)*
*Because this book is in black and white, the blue pieces are shown as black, the green as white and the king as grey.

1) Lay the pieces on the board as shown.

2) The attackers try to capture the king, while the defenders help the king escape.

3) Attackers go first. Each player takes turns. You can move your piece as far as you want along any straight line, the way a rook moves in chess.

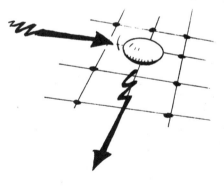

Nobody but the king can sit on the throne square, though pieces can pass through it.

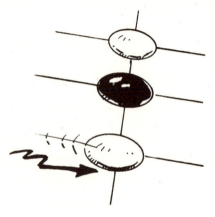

4) Pieces are captured by flanking them on two sides, like this:

This is called a 'capturing party'.

5) If a piece moves between

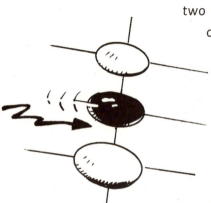

two pieces belonging to the other team, that piece is not captured – the capturing party must capture a piece of the opposing team by flanking it, but it cannot be captured by moving into a flanked position.

Corner spaces are safe from capture as you cannot get pieces either side. Maybe these are 'hiding places'.

6) For the attackers to win, they have to surround the king on all four sides, like this:

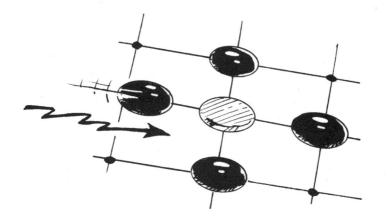

... unless the king is on a space right next to the throne, when it takes only three attackers to capture him as no piece other than the king can sit in the throne space.

7) In order for the defenders to win, they have to help the king escape to the edge of the board.

8) Another way to win is for your opponent just to give up! This is probably how most games were won.

Hurling was a popular sport in Celtic times and was talked about in the epics. Warriors such as Cú Chulainn played it, as did Fionn Mac Cumhaill. The modern game is tough, but ancient hurling makes it look like a tickling competition in comparison. It's thought that a friendly match might have involved several dozen participants and would often erupt into lethal violence. Nothing new there, but some evidence suggests the game may sometimes have been played with severed human heads!

STORYTELLING

Storytelling was an important way of not just killing time on long, cold, winter nights, but of passing tales on to future generations. The Celts never wrote anything down, and information was transferred by word of mouth. Extra bits may have been added by inventive storytellers as the years passed, so a bit of exaggeration might have crept into the stories. But the Celts loved exaggeration, so that was okay! Their tales, which we'll go into later, were full of magic and the supernatural as well as impossible feats of strength and agility. A bit like a modern superhero movie, but where you had to use your imagination instead of relying on flashy special effects.

Now we know what the Celts did all year, let's find out what they liked to wear. They might not have had catwalks and supermodels back in Celtic times, but if they did, they might have looked something like this …

FASHION WEEK IN CELTIC IRELAND

JUST BECAUSE YOU'RE OUT *SPLITTING SKULLS* ALL DAY, DOESN'T MEAN YOU CAN'T LOOK *SENSATIONAL* DOING IT!

CAOIMHÍN IS SIMPLY *STUNNING* IN THE CLASSIC LÉINE/BRAT* COMBO! NOTE THE SHORT-SLEEVED *LÉINE* GATHERED AT THE WAIST BY A LEATHER BELT AND MATCHING *SHOES*.

*LÉINE – LONG LINEN SHIRT
BRAT – WOOLLEN CLOAK

CHECK OUT THE PATTERNED *BRACCAE** PULLED TIGHT AT THE ANKLES AND THE LONG BRAT HELD IN PLACE AT THE SHOULDER WITH A GOLD BROOCH!

HE TOPS THE *NOBLE WARRIOR* LOOK OFF WITH A SHIMMERING GOLD NECK TORC AND MATCHING ARM-RING. *PURE CLASS!*

I MUST SAY, CAOIMHÍN'S HAIR LOOKS *AWESOME*, WASHED IN LIME AND PULLED BACK SO IT'S *HARDENED* INTO LONG SPIKES!

**BRACCAE – WOOLLEN TROUSERS

DON'T FORGET HIS LONG MOUSTACHE THE ROMANS CALLED THE *'WINE STRAINER'*! VERY FEW GUYS CAN *ROCK THAT LOOK* BUT CAOIMHÍN PULLS IT OFF WITH *STYLE!*

55

Believe it or not, some Celtic warriors really did charge into battle naked to show how brave they were by not wearing any armour. Let's see what other weird warrior ways the Celts practised ...

ONE FOR THE WOAD

WEAPONS AND WAR

More than eating, more than celebrating, more than playing fidchell, and more than looking good, the Celts just loved a good fight. A young man's training in the ways of war started very early on.

Here are some DEADLY! DATA battle cards to show you the kinds of weapons a Celtic boy would have had to learn how to use and train with daily.

SWORD (CLOIDEM)

Only wealthy warriors could afford a sword and the more elaborately decorated the sword and scabbard, the wealthier you were. The blade was made from iron and the hilt (handle) could be made from wood, bronze, copper alloy or a combination of materials.

LENGTH: 60 CM
WEIGHT: 0.7 KG
EASE OF USE: 4
DEADLINESS: 6

FATAL FACT: Irish swords were quite short and were used for hacking and stabbing in close combat.

Deadly!

Battle Cards

SHIELD (SCIATH)

There were many different Celtic shields, from tiny round ones to big rectangular and oval ones. Usually made with yew-wood covered with leather hardened with chalk or lime and brightly painted, they got bashed to pieces quite easily.

LENGTH: 50 CM
WEIGHT: 3.5 KG
EASE OF USE: 9
DEADLINESS: 3

FATAL FACT: The metal boss in the centre not only protected the warrior's hand, but could also be used to bash an enemy's nose.

SPEAR (GAE)

Spears were the main weapons Celtic Irish warriors used. There were two kinds: thrusting and throwing, with the throwing spear being the shorter and lighter of the two. The heads were made of bronze or iron with a hollow socket held by rivets.

LENGTH: 200 CM
WEIGHT: 0.9 KG
EASE OF USE: 6
DEADLINESS: 7

FATAL FACT: Some throwing spears had a loop called a suaineamh attached to the handle where the forefinger was inserted. This helped the spear go further.

ARMOUR (CATHÉIDE)

Some Irish Celtic warriors took pride in not wearing any armour into battle, but others did wear it. Armour was made of leather and later, chainmail. This was a shirt made of thousands of tiny metal rings linked together.

LENGTH: 75 CM

WEIGHT: 10 KG

EASE OF USE: 5

DEADLINESS: 2

FATAL FACT: The Celts are thought to have invented chainmail, but only rich warriors could afford it.

SLING (TAILM)

They don't look like much, but don't be fooled – these rope and leather slings were lethal in the right hands. They took a lot of practice to master, but it's said Celtic Irish warriors could part an enemy's hair from 100 metres away.

LENGTH: 183 CM

WEIGHT: 0.3 KG

EASE OF USE: 3

DEADLINESS: 8

FATAL FACT: Warriors used smooth, round stones which they kept in a bag on their belt. They also kept a larger hand-stone in their shields as a back-up weapon.

HELMET (CAFFAR)

Some Celtic warriors went into battle with their hair pulled back into long spikes, but many wore helmets of leather reinforced with metal bars. Others wore iron helmets with flowing horse-hair plumes or with metal animals and birds.

LENGTH: 48 CM

WEIGHT: 3 KG

EASE OF USE: 10

DEADLINESS: 1

FATAL FACT: It was actually the Celts who wore horns on their helmets, not the Vikings.

Those were the more everyday weapons the Irish Celts used, but in the stories about their gods and heroes, there were some very exotic implements of war that may or may not have been real ...

WEAPON OR NO WEAPON

WELCOME BACK TO *WEAPON OR NO WEAPON,* FOLKS! HERE WE HAVE THREE BOXES, EACH OF WHICH CONTAINS ... YOU'VE GUESSED IT – A *WEAPON.*

IT'S UP TO CONCHÚR, OUR *LUCKY* CONTESTANT, TO DECIDE IF IT'S ONE THE IRISH CELTS TALKED ABOUT IN THEIR *STORIES.*

IF HE GUESSES RIGHT, HE'LL WIN *LOTS OF GOLD.* IF HE DOESN'T, HE'LL BE PUT TO *DEATH.* READY, CONCHÚR?

ER ... I S'POSE ...

IN BOX NUMBER ONE, WE HAVE *LUGH'S SPEAR* – A LIVING WEAPON THAT THIRSTED FOR BLOOD AND COULD FLY ALL BY ITSELF.

IN BOX NUMBER TWO, WE HAVE THE *TATHLUM* – A CONCRETE BALL MADE FROM THE BRAINS OF DEAD ENEMIES MIXED WITH BLOOD AND LIME.

AND FINALLY IN BOX NUMBER THREE, WE HAVE THE *GAE BOLGA* – A SPEAR WITH DEADLY BARBS ALONG THE SIDES WHICH MEANT IT HAD TO BE CUT OUT OF A WOUND.

61

A DEADLY! GUIDE TO ...
CATTLE RAIDING

As king of your tribe, you have decided you'd like a few more cattle to add to your collection as well as some more slaves, so you order a raid on a neighbouring tribe. And you've taken quite a fancy to that rather nice neck torc you saw the rival king wear at a meeting a few months ago. Great! It must be three whole weeks since you had a good fight ...

1) You 'muster the hosts', where you call all your warriors. The last one to arrive is not only a rotten egg, he might be tortured to death in front of everyone to make sure no one's late next time!*

2) March your warriors, who are armed with swords, shields and spears, to the nearby rival settlement. You ride in your two-wheeled battle chariot,** driven by your charioteer. You like to show off by running up and down the yoke-pole between the horses.

---

* What we know about Celtic warfare is taken from accounts by their enemies and from the sagas. Practices like the ones described here probably didn't happen EVERY time. At least, I hope not!
** Although evidence of chariots has not been found in Ireland, it's likely the Celts used them as they're mentioned in the old tales.

3) Your enemies know you're coming because they built their roundhouses on an open plain with a good view of the countryside. They come out to meet you, and your men try to scare the bejapers out of them by banging their weapons against their shields, shouting, singing, blowing horns and beating drums.

4) You've been practising some new insults,* so you shout at the rival king, 'Large as the head of a cow will your dung be when you flee from the sight of me!' He shouts back, 'My sword will give your belly a red smile this day!' This goes back and forth until both armies are well riled up!

* We'll see how to do great warrior insults a bit later!

5) Don't fly into battle just yet – get your greatest warrior to challenge your rival's greatest warrior and watch them go at it. It might seem daft to risk your best fighter, but we Celts aren't afraid of death, and being slain in battle is the best way to die!

6) Your champion has badly wounded his rival, which gives your men courage, and the two armies rush wildly at each other. Your charioteer drives you into the middle of the action, where you skewer a few of your enemies with your spears. When you get close to the rival king, leap off your chariot and challenge him to a sword-fight.

7) Wear him down by slicing, hacking and slashing at him. Make sure to hurl plenty of insults at him about his mother. Get him mad enough so he gets careless and you find a weakness.

8) You batter your rival to the ground, but just as you raise your sword to cut off his head, he swings a dagger round and sticks you right between the ribs!

9) When your warriors see you fall, they lose heart and flee. The battle is over. Your rival smiles down at you as your blood seeps into the ground. Then he cuts your head off to keep as a trophy.

10) Your rival's men start collecting the heads of your dead warriors as well as their weapons and jewellery. Later, he will go to your settlement and take slaves and cattle. Then afterwards he'll have a feast in his roundhouse to celebrate his victory, whilst wearing that nice torc of yours he saw round your neck at a meeting a few months ago ...

So what exactly did Celts want all those severed heads for?

The Celts' head-hunting ways were just one of the reasons why the Greeks and Romans thought of them as barbarians. They didn't understand that there was a reason why these fierce warriors loved heads so much. Apart from showing others how brilliant they were in battle by collecting the heads of their enemies, the Celts believed that the head contained the soul of the person and would live in it even after it had been removed from the body. They thought the head then became protective of its new owner and would pass on knowledge from the Otherworld – the Celtic afterlife.

The Celts liked to celebrate victories and special occasions with a big feast. Now, you'd think there'd be nothing nicer than sitting around with friends, eating, drinking and having a bit of craic, but the Celts would use even these feasts as an excuse for more fighting. This was because the warriors would argue over who deserved the *Curadhmír* – the Hero's Portion – which was the best bit of meat. The Hero's Portion is mentioned often in the Irish sagas, like in The Story of Mac Dá Tho's Pig (*Scéla Mucce Meic Dathó*), which features a swine of rather epic size …

THE WARRIORS OF ULSTER AND CONNACHT ARE GUESTS AT MAC DÁ THO'S FEAST IN LEINSTER AND, AS USUAL, A ROW BREAKS OUT OVER WHO SHOULD GET THE CURADHMÍR...

I AM CET MAC MÁGACH – CONNACHT'S GREATEST WARRIOR – AND I SHOULD GET THE HERO'S PORTION!

NO WAY! THE CURADHMÍR IS MINE, CET!

OHH, HAVE YOU FORGOTTEN ABOUT THE DAY I CUT YOUR FATHER'S HANDS OFF IN BATTLE, ÓENGUS?

WELL, ME DA SURE HASN'T FORGOTTEN. HE HAS TO USE HIS TOES TO COUNT TO TEN NOW.

7... 8...

AND REMEMBER HOW I PUT YOUR EYE OUT AT A CATTLE-RAID, ÉOGAN?

EYE – EYE DO!

AND DID I NOT SLICE YOUR FATHER'S FOOT CLEAN OFF, MEND?

HE'S HOPPING MAD ABOUT IT, CET.

@)#*★!!

BOING BOING

SO ARE WE ALL AGREED I GET THE CURADHMÍR BECAUSE I'M CLA, QUITE FRANKLY, AND YOUSE ARE ALL USELESS?

AYE, S'POSE.

68

69

We've just met Cet Mac Mágach and, as you know, he likes to boast and brag. But does he tell lies as well? **Answers below.**

A) I NAIL THE HEADS OF MY DEFEATED ENEMIES ABOVE THE DOOR OF MY ROUNDHOUSE.

C) THE MORRIGAN, GODDESS OF WAR, CAN SHAPESHIFT INTO A CROW.

B) WE CELTS BELIEVE OUR SOULS COME BACK INTO NEW BODIES AFTER WE DIE.

D) THE IRISH CELTS WERE THE FIRST PEOPLE IN EUROPE TO HAVE HOSPITALS.

ANSWERS: Cet may be a loudmouth, but he wasn't lying! a) Yep. Celts like to show off their heads the way we like to show off a new car. Warriors would even talk to their heads like they were pets! b) True. They believed they went to the Otherworld when they died then came back again after a while. c) She certainly can. More about her later. d) Uh-huh. Queen Macha Mong Ruadh built Bróin Bherg, 'House of Sorrows', at Eamhain Mhacha, near Armagh. After, every region in Ireland had its own hospital to tend the sick and wounded.

DEADLY! CRAFTY INSULT GENERATOR

When in combat, you have to fight not only with your weapons, but also your tongue! Irish Celt warriors taunted and insulted their enemies before, during and after a battle, a bit like how boxers and MMA fighters trash-talk each other today.

This was an art in itself. It wasn't just a matter of saying, 'You smell bad', you had to use a bit of imagination. To get you started, pick one phrase from each column and mix them up to make some great insults and taunts that will make your foes run crying to mammy.

	A	B	C	
Your	mother	has a face like	burnt thatch	
	sister	loves to eat	week-old milk	
	father	wears	a baby's nappy	
	brother	has a head like	cold porridge	*and*
you fight like a	sick	squirrel	with two broken legs	
	dead	chicken	with the pox	
	blind	sheep	with no head	
	drowned	duck	with a smelly bottom	*and*
Your	sword	is only fit for	a pretendy fight!	
	spear	is only good for	a baby's toy!	
	chariot	is only useful for	the dung heap!	

WARRIOR WOMEN

Roman writers mention how fierce Celtic women were on the battlefield. Women warriors were common in Irish Celtic society and one story tells how the mighty Cú Chulainn was trained by a woman named Scáthach, whose name means *The Shadowy One*.

If you wanted the honour of being trained by Scáthach, you had to find her first, crossing stormy seas and treacherous rocks to reach her Fortress of Shadows, Dún Scáith, on the Isle of Skye in Scotland. Once there, you had to get past Scáthach's daughter, Uathach, who guarded the gates. (Cú Chulainn did his mighty salmon leap to get into the fortress.) Even then, there was always the chance warriors wouldn't survive being trained by the ferocious warrior woman.

What happened to Scáthach? Eventually she became a Celtic goddess ... of the DEAD!

72

YOU CAN'T MYTH THIS
MYTHS AND LEGENDS

The *Leabhar Gabhála* or The Book of Invasions tells the mythological history of Ireland, which gives a different account from the one modern historians tell. It says that Ireland was invaded by six different tribes: the Cessair, the Parthalón, the Nemed, the Fir Bolg, the Tuatha Dé Danann and the Milesians. The first four tribes were destroyed or forced to leave, while the Tuatha Dé Danann became Ireland's pagan gods and the Milesians became the Irish people or Gaels.

The *Tuatha Dé Danann* were kind of like a superhero team, each with their own special powers.

DEADLY! TDD* DATABASE

NAME: The Dagda, father of the gods
GOD OF: Agriculture, strength, magic and wisdom
POWERS: Dagda's club can kill and restore life! His harp can alter time! His cauldron never runs dry!

NAME: Lugh of the Long Arm
GOD OF: The sun, thunderstorms, arts and crafts
POWERS: Lugh is master of many skills. He has a magical hound called Failinis, enchanted weapons and a horse that can travel over land and sea.

* Tuatha Dé Danann

74

NAME: The Morrigan
GODDESS OF: War and fate
POWERS: Flight, shape-shifting, foretelling the future, ability to cause confusion.

NAME: Nuada of the Silver Arm
GOD OF: Healing, warfare, youth, writing, sorcery
POWERS: Nuada lost an arm in a battle and had it replaced by a silver arm. He also owns the invincible Sword of Light that can cut people in half!

NAME: Manannán Mac Lir
GOD OF: The sea and the otherworld
POWERS: Manannán owns a magical boat and chariot, a powerful sword and a cloak of invisibility.

Every superhero team has supervillains to battle and the TDD were no different. They fought against the Fomorians, fiendish creatures from beneath the earth and sea. They were a bunch of bullies who unfairly taxed the people of Ireland and caused famines and drought.

The Fomorian leader was Balor of the Evil Eye. It took four men just to lift his eyelid and when his eye was opened, it destroyed everything it gazed upon. (A bit like that look your ma gives you when you haven't tidied your room.)

The god Lugh put Balor's eye out at the second battle of Moytura and ended his tyrannical rule over Ireland.

HOW CÚ CHULAINN GOT HIS NAME

Cú Chulainn was the son of the sun god, Lugh, which made him half-human, half-god, and there were many tales about him. He wasn't always called Cú Chulainn, though. Here's how he got his name.

78

AND THAT'S HOW SETANTA BECAME *CÚ CHULAINN* – THE HOUND OF CULANN.

Shaking with rage, massively muscled, legs twisted backwards, one eye sucked deep into his head, the other eye popped completely out, cheeks pulled so far back you can see his internal organs flapping about, hair giving off sparks and spiked so sharply it could skewer apples, blood gushing out of the head …

No, it's not your big brother when he's found you've eaten the last of the corn flakes. It's Cú Chulainn having a *riastradh* or 'warp-spasm' when he gets so furiously angry on the battlefield he changes from handsome, noble, virtuous warrior into a monstrous, rampaging, terrifyingly ugly killing-machine!

Cú Chulainn gets so worked up when he's in this state that he kills EVERYBODY in his path, including warriors on his own side, so best not to get him angry. You wouldn't like him when he's angry.

THE SALMON OF KNOWLEDGE

Another Celtic hero was Fionn Mac Cumhaill or Finn McCool, leader of the Fianna warriors. The most famous story about Fionn is the time he helped a druid called Finnegas catch a magical salmon. Whoever ate the fish was supposed to gain all the knowledge of the world, and Finnegas wanted this more than anything. Fionn cooked the Salmon of Knowledge for Finnegas but burned his thumb on it. He stuck his thumb in his mouth to ease the pain, and it was Fionn, not Finnegas who gained all the knowledge in the world. Any time he wanted to know anything, all he had to do was suck his thumb. An example of the ancient Celtic internet.

Fionn was once tricked by an evil old hag to jump into a lake at the top of a mountain called Slieve Gullion in Co. Armagh, which turned  him into an old man. She eventually turned him young again, but his hair remained forever white, which is why some people called him Fionn the Fair.

A CELTIC BESTIARY*

There are many bizarre creatures which inhabit Celtic Irish folklore – some are friendly and others not so much. Here are just a few.

CROM CRUACH –
Ancient worm god

ɛLAS GAIBHNENN – A cow with green spots that produces vast quantities of milk

LAIGNECH FALEAD – Irish werewolves

BANSHEE – A spirit who foretells death

SLUAGH – dark spirits who prey on the souls of the dying

MERROW – Irish merfolk

MARBH BHEO – Irish zombies

OLLIPHEIST – Lake-dwelling dragon

* A bestiary is a book of beasts

Have YOU got what it takes to be one of Fionn Mac Cumhaill's Fianna warriors?

IF YOU CAN …

1. Learn 12 books of poetry off by heart.
2. Stand in a hole up to your waist and, using only a shield and a hazel stick, defend against nine warriors, without getting wounded.

3. Run through a forest while being chased by warriors without breaking a single twig or tearing your clothes or snagging your hair braid on a branch.
4. Jump over a branch as tall as yourself.

5. Run under a stick placed at knee-height.
6. Pick a thorn from your foot while running at top speed.

… THEN WE WANT TO HEAR FROM YOU! CALL OUR RECRUITMENT OFFICE ON 555-9124 TO SIGN UP NOW!

BEALTAINE ALONG NICELY

RELIGION

The Celts had priests and priestesses called druids, who were in charge of all religious affairs. The druids had secret knowledge, such as the important dates of the year – the feast days, solstices and equinoxes – and ways of pleasing the gods, some of which were pretty gruesome. They were schooled for twenty years, where they had to memorise everything by heart – poetry, astronomy, magic, astrology, medicine, law and science. The druids never wrote anything down, so some of what we know about them comes from Julius Caesar who conquered Britain in 54 BCE. He said of the druids:

THE GODS DELIGHT IN THE SLAUGHTER OF PRISONERS AND CRIMINALS, AND WHEN THE SUPPLY OF CAPTIVES RUNS SHORT, THEY SACRIFICE EVEN THE INNOCENT.

THOUGH IT'S HARD TO FIND ANYONE WHO'S *INNOCENT* IN THIS DAY AND AGE!

It is not known if the druids in Ireland made human sacrifices, but it seems likely. Some bodies found in bogs around Ireland and Britain dating from the Celtic era suggest they may have been killed to please the gods. There was a bog body found in Clonycavan, Co. Meath, who looked like he'd been sacrificed. He had nicely groomed hair with expensive gel* in it, so it is possible he was an important person like a king.

Why would the druids have done this? They may have sacrificed their king if there was a bad harvest as the Celts believed the king and land were one and the same. Another reason may have been for divination purposes – for 'telling the future'.

* The hair gel was made from plant oil and pine resin imported from France and Spain.

The Greek historian Diodorus Siculus said that the druids 'choose a person for death and stab him or her in the chest above the diaphragm. By the convulsion of the victim's limbs and the spurting of blood, they foretell the future.'

Although this is all very ghastly to our modern eyes, sacrifice – mostly of animals – was an essential part of worship. But other things were 'sacrificed' too – precious things like swords and jewellery. Keeping the gods happy was the number one priority, otherwise your next battle might end badly, you might be struck down by sickness or your hens might start laying their eggs funny. Everything was an omen – a sign from the gods – to the Celts.

THE RULE OF THREE

The Celts seemed to be fascinated with the number three, believing it had magical qualities. Their gods and goddesses were often three-in-one beings, like the Earth goddess Danu, who could appear as a beautiful young maiden, a mother or an old crone. There is a stone head in the National Museum in Dublin that has three faces, which may depict a god or goddess, gazing into the past, present and future all at once.

Spirals have special significance to the Celts and some rock carvings and jewellery has been found with patterns of three spirals. When you think about it, the number three is still special today. Most of our fairy tales have three things in them and things happening in threes. In Goldilocks and the Three Bears, for instance, Goldilocks eats from three bowls, sits on three chairs and lies in three beds. (If she'd done that in my house, there'd be three knocks from three cops who'd give her three seconds to get out of my house and stop stealing my stuff!)

The thing about the Celts' religion was that, for them, it was everywhere, not just in a place you went to once a week for half an hour. They saw magic, omens and the supernatural in the trees and birds, in the weather and the sea and the sky.

To show how serious they were about their religion, the druids ordered the building of an impressive circular temple at Eamhain Mhacha (near Armagh) in 95 BCE. At 40 m in diameter, it took many months, possibly even years to build.

Here's how the Celts did it ...

A DEADLY! GUIDE TO...

BUILDING THE TEMPLE AT EAMHAIN MHACHA

1) Cut down a giant oak tree, trim the branches and make it into a central pillar 12 m high and weighing a whopping 3,600 kg. Put this into a hole 2 m deep.

2) Chop down another 280 smaller oak trees to make 5 circles radiating outwards from the centre, like a cartwheel. Make four aisles and an entrance facing west.

3) Put up timber walls and a thatched roof so it's like a giant roundhouse.

4) Call everyone from far and wide with ceremonial trumpets for your religious ceremony inside, dedicated to the local goddess, Macha.

5) Fill it with thousands of limestone boulders, making a mound almost 3m high.

6) Set fire to the whole lot. That's right, burn that sucker down.

7) When the fire's out, cover the mound with soil and turf.

Seems like a lot of work for a building that was used maybe only once. Remember there were no diggers, tractors or bulldozers back then, which means all the work had to be done by humans and animals putting in a huge amount of effort.

Historians are not actually 100% certain what Eamhain Mhacha was used for, but they've made educated guesses. It could have been an offering to the gods and was sacrificed to them by being burned and buried. Or it could've been created as a portal to the Otherworld where the druids could contact gods and spirits. The truth is we don't know and probably never will. But if you go there today, over 2,000 years later, you can still feel the magic and mystery crackling in the air.

This is Fidelma the Druidess. Don't let the way she looks scare you – she's a pussycat really. She may be a religious woman, but is she 'holy' honest?

Answers below.

A) WE DRUIDS MAKE A GIANT WICKER FIGURE, STUFF IT WITH CRIMINALS AND NE'ER-DO-WELLS, THEN SET FIRE TO IT AS A SACRIFICE TO THE GODS.

B) THE SKULL OF A BARBARY APE WAS FOUND AT EAMHAIN MHACHA.

C) DRUIDS BUILT ALL THE MEGALITHIC STANDING STONES AROUND IRELAND.

D) SAINT PATRICK GOT RID OF ALL THE DRUIDS IN IRELAND.

ANSWERS: Fidelma is a bit of a fibber. a) Perhaps. Julius Caesar and others said they witnessed this in Britain, but some historians say it was made up to make the druids look bad. b) True. This type of ape is only found in Africa. So how did it get there? c) Nope. The megaliths were there long before the druids. d) Not exactly. Some people think the legend of Saint Patrick driving all the snakes out of Ireland actually meant driving all the druids out, but the druids' religion carried on through the Christian era.

THOSE CRAFTY CELTS
ART AND CULTURE

When they weren't fighting each other, the Celts took the time to make beautiful art. Most art took the form of decoration on objects that let people know about the owner's wealth and status. A rich warrior, for example, might hire a skilled craftworker to add jewels to the hilt of his sword and matching scabbard, similar to the way car enthusiasts add spoilers, xenon lights and fluffy dice to their automobiles. Most Celts were show-offs ... just like an eejit I know who has a yoke that looks like something from a sci-fi film yet can't go over a speed bump at more than one mile an hour. But hey, each to their own!

European Celts had an art style called Hallstatt, which had a spiky, angular feel to it, but that style never reached Ireland. Instead, most art objects found in Ireland were decorated in a style called La Tène, after a place in Switzerland. This style used spirals, waves and curves, and has an elegant, stylish look. Because iron corrodes over time and gold was rare, most art items that have been found are bronze.

They didn't have fancy auction houses back in Celtic times, but if they did, a catalogue might have looked something like this ...

CELTIE'S AUCTION HOUSE

SINCE 700 BCE

Ardnaglug Collar, Co. Roscommon. 3rd century BCE. Gold collar decorated with spirals and S-shapes. The earliest example of La Tène art in Ireland. Probably imported from Europe.

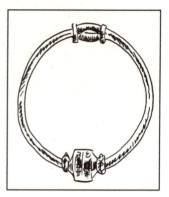

Petrie Crown, Co. Cork. 200–100 BCE. Bronze head-dress with hollow cone-shaped horns and circular discs, decorated with triskeles (spiral designs), birds' heads and beads.

Turoe Stone, Co. Galway. 100 BCE–AD 100. Granite stone decorated with spirals. Likely used in religious ceremonies.

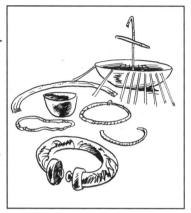

Broighter Hoard, Co. Derry. First century BCE. Gold objects consisting of a bowl, torcs, necklaces and a little boat complete with teeny-weeny oars, a mast, a rudder, rowing benches, tools and a spear. Possibly an offering to the sea-god Manannán Mac Lir.

Loughnashade Trumpet, Co. Armagh. 100 BCE. Two-metre long bronze trumpet found near the royal centre of Eamhain Mhacha. Could have been used as a war trumpet and in religious ceremonies.

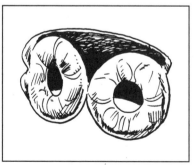

Newry Armlet, Co. Down. AD 100. Bronze arm-ring. Imported from eastern Scotland.

OᵹHAM ON NOW!
WRITINᵹ

The Celts never wrote anything down, choosing instead to memorise their knowledge and stories and pass them down through the generations by word of mouth. But they still had a system of writing called Ogham (pronounced 'oh-am') and the experts hotly debate just how old the Ogham alphabet is. Some say it dates back to the fifth or sixth century AD while others argue it is up to 2,500 years old.

Legend has it that it was created by the Irish god Ogma mac Elathen, one of the Tuatha Dé Danann and Lord of Knowledge, who, like all good inventors, called it after himself. However, some historians believe it started out as a secret sign language created by the druids in Europe.

Each letter was named after a tree, which were sacred to the Celts, which is why Ogham is often called the Celtic Tree Alphabet. Here's how Ogham looked:

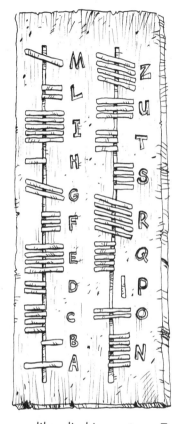

Because they were straight lines, the letters were easy to carve along a central line on wood, or chisel on the edge of a stone. Around 300 Ogham stones dot the Irish landscape, though it's not certain what they were used for. Some historians think they acted as gravestones, border markers or even as legal documents. One of them reads, 'Belonging to the Three Sons of the Bald One'. Another says, 'He Who Was Born Of The Raven.' Don't look at me! I don't know either.

Unlike our alphabet, which runs from left to right, Ogham goes from bottom to top, a bit like climbing a tree. Try writing your name in Ogham. (Because there were only twenty letters in the Ogham alphabet, you will have to make up your own letters if j, k, v, w, x or y appear in your name.) Then translate what these three Ogham stones say. Start at the bottom of the first stone, work your way upwards, then start at the bottom of the next stone.

Answers below.

The first mention of Ogham in the ancient Irish tales was when when Ogma Mac Elathen sent the god Lugh a message of a birch rod with seven strokes carved into it, each representing the letter 'B'.

Now, if I received this message I'd be totally clueless as to what it meant, but Lugh, being a god and all that, understood it to mean that the Sidhe, or faeries, were planning to kidnap his wife unless she was protected with birch. Aw, okay then.

In the *Táin Bó Cúailnge* (The Cattle Raid of Cooley), Cú Chulainn wrote an Ogham message by bending an oak sapling into a hoop and securing it with a wooden peg on which he wrote the message. He challenged the reader of the message to copy his feat. Sounds easy enough, but good aul Cú Chulainn did this by using just one arm, with one eye closed while standing on one leg!

In the tale *Tochmarc Étaíne*, (The Wooing of Étaín), a druid called Dalan takes four wands made of yew wood, and writes three Ogham letters on each. He then uses these as tools for divination (telling the future) to find a beautiful woman called Étaín who was taken by the sidhe king Midir. Sounds like there was an awful lot of ladies being kidnapped by faeries going on back then!

A book written in the 14th century called the Leabhar Bhaile an Mhóta or the Book of Ballymote goes into a lot of detail about Ogham, giving 150 different versions of the Ogham alphabet that had to be learned during the first three years of a bard's training. (Bards were professional storytellers.) I don't know about you, but I don't think I would have made it as a bard. Learning one alphabet is difficult enough, thank you very much! Or should I say, thank *yew* very much.

DEADLY! CRAFTY OGHAM STONE

1) Get a long, thin cardboard box. Tape a square of card over the top and tape flaps onto the bottom.

2) Tear loads of newspaper or magazine pages into strips. (It doesn't matter if your ma or da hasn't read it yet — they'll just be happy you're making things.)

3) Make some paper mache (or papier-mâché if you're posh) paste with water and glue mixed together in a bowl. About half glue/half water.

4) Dip a strip of newspaper into the paste. Run your fingers down the strip to remove excess paste. This helps stop the paper from being too soggy and fragile.

5) Stick the strips of paper all over the box.

6) Crumple up loads more of the newspaper strips, dip in the paper mache paste and add a second layer over the first – to give a stony texture.

CRUMPLE!

7) Let the paper mache dry for 24 hours in a warm but well-ventilated area. If it feels soggy, it's not ready yet.

8) Once the paper mache is dry, glue or tape the bottom flaps onto a piece of card to form a base. Paint the flaps and base green, to look like grass.

GLUE

9) Paint the box grey. You are going for a stone-like effect. You could dapple it with the paintbrush or use different shades of grey.

10) To make it look even more realistic, get an old toothbrush (or use your sister's – she won't mind) and flick some white paint onto the stone with your thumb.

11) Write an Ogham message along the edges of the stone with a marker, and display with pride!

BREHON AND ON AND ON ...
LAW AND PUNISHMENT

Imagine you lived in a world where the ultimate goal was fairness, peace and harmony. Where there was no need for police or prisons. Where whoever came to your door must be fed, no questions asked. These were the laws the Celts were expected to live by – the Brehon laws.

A *breitheamh* or *brehon* (someone who specialised in the law) had to memorise tons of legal knowledge, and like the druids, bards, poets and seers, he was thought to possess magical powers. A brehon called Morann wore a magical collar round his neck that tightened when he gave a false judgement and loosened again when he gave the true one.

Telling the truth was a matter of honour to the Celts and was seen as a great virtue.

When someone broke the law, they had to pay a fine, and if they couldn't pay, their immediate family were expected to pay. If they couldn't pay, the wider family were next in line. If no one could pay, the accused person could be killed or taken into slavery, so this meant it was in everyone's interests to stay on the right side of the law.

Sometimes people refused to accept a judgement against them, especially if they were of a higher rank than their accuser. In cases like this, the accuser could, by law, sit outside the house of the accused from dawn until dusk and refuse to eat. By custom, the accused could not eat either or else they might lose their honour and no proud Celt wanted that.

The Brehon laws lasted from Celtic times all the way up to the 17th century and were one of the oldest law systems in the world. Although they were mostly fair, we might find some of them a bit strange today.

It is illegal to give somebody food in which has been found a dead mouse or weasel.

(So dead rats and stoats are okay then?)

When you become old, your family must provide you with one oatcake a day plus a container of sour milk. They must bathe you every 20th night and wash your head every Saturday. Seventeen sticks of firewood is the allotment for keeping you warm.

(Oatcakes? Sour milk? YECCCHH! No, thanks!)

Some of the more famous Brehon judgements have lasted through the mists of time and exist today as Irish proverbs.

Many a time a man's mouth broke his nose.

Everyone is wise until he speaks.

If your enemy offends you, buy each of his kids a drum kit.*

Of all the Brehon laws, one was taken most seriously – the geasa or taboo. A taboo is something you're not allowed to do. For instance, after he killed Culann's hound, Cú Chulainn swore a geasa never to eat dog-flesh. You'd think this would be pretty easy to do – I've never eaten dog myself and I can't imagine it tasting great – but Cú Chulainn managed to break his geasa when a witch tricked him into it, a bit like how Fionn Mac Cumhaill was tricked into swimming in a lake that would make him grow old.

*Okay, I made that one up.

FERDIA AND DEIRDRE
CELTIC KIDS AND FAMILIES

It might surprise you to know that back in Celtic times, most children were not brought up by their own families. Boys and girls were sent at a young age to live with a foster family, and didn't return home for years. Young Ferdia and teenager Deirdre will tell you all about it.

Ferdia's Diary: I had to get up before sunrise to start our long journey north. My dad, who's the king, is driving me in his chariot to my new foster home, which is far away in a place called *Eamhain Mhacha*. We will travel the *Slighe Midluachra*, one of the five great roads. I'm excited, but also sad. Mum wailed with sorrow as we were leaving, and my aunts had to hold her, but I puffed out my chest and did not look back as I knew I would cry if I did. And young warriors don't cry.

Deirdre's Diary: I have been dreading this day for ages. Although my foster-brother Cian was eager to start the long journey south on the Slighe Midluachra, I could not leave until I had hugged every single member of my foster-family — even the dogs! It's amazing to think I've been with these kind people for seven years, but now I must return home, for I am turning fourteen and I am to be married. That is what the law says. I hope and pray to see my lovely muimme* and my foster-brothers and sisters again, but I may not. Someone who I will never see again in this life is my poor, brave aite*. He was killed a few years ago and it was all because of me. I'm crying now, just thinking about it.

* **muimme** and **aite** — foster mum and dad.

F: Slighe Midluachra is NOT a great road! It's just a bunch of planks and stones laid out in the mud! Talk about disappointing. *SHEESH!* Dad has been telling me stories about the place I am going to. He says we will be travelling through Táin Bó Cúailnge country where Cú Chulainn once lived! I love that story, especially the bit where Cú Chulainn goes nuts and has his *riastradh!* *GRAAAARRRR!* I am called after Cú Chulainn's best friend and foster-brother Ferdia who was a great warrior but who Cú Chulainn had to kill. I keep thinking about my new foster-family. Will I like them? Will they like me? Will any of my foster-brothers want to kill <u>me</u>?!

113

D: Slighe Midluachra is such an awesome road. As we travelled along, I thought about the people who built it. I try not to think about leaving my dear foster family behind as it just makes me sad, but I am looking forward to returning home. I keep wondering if my own family will recognise me. My wee brothers and sisters won't — they were just babies and toddlers when I left. Will I recognise Mum and Dad? They must be a right old age now — in their thirties!

F: We passed some fianna warriors on the road. They looked a bit scraggly and hungry and we thought they might be *díbheargaigh* — bandits — and would try to steal our stuff. But Dad gave them 'the look' and they just passed on by. I hope 'the look' is one of the things I will be taught in my warrior training at my new home, but I don't think anyone can do 'the look' as well as my dad.

D: We made camp for the night just off the road. Cian caught a trout with his fishing-spear in a nearby river, and I cooked it, along with some vegetables we'd brought with us. Cooking was just one of the skills my dear foster-mother taught me. Being the daughter of a king, I had to learn other skills as well, like sewing and embroidery. Cian thinks it's strange that my father did not come to fetch me himself, but I tell him my father is a very busy man. But secretly, I agree with him.

F: Dad killed a wood pigeon with his slingshot and we had it for supper. Dad's cooking isn't anyway near as good as Mum's – he left half the feathers on – but it was nice enough. We talked about lots of things, but the one thing we didn't talk about was my sister who was fostered when I was little. A couple of years ago a messenger was sent out to us to say she'd been taken in a cattle-raid. She is probably a slave somewhere now, or worse still, dead. Mum and Dad don't talk of her. I don't really remember her, but I do remember a doll she had that Dad had made for her. It had a wooden body with straw for hair and wore a checked dress. How do I remember some stupid doll and not my own sister?

D: We set off early in the morning after a light breakfast of leftover trout and bread. But when we were trying to get back up onto the road, one of the chariot wheels buckled and tossed us both out! Now my face and dress are all covered in mud! I look a right state! Cian's father — my foster-father — always told him to look after his chariot and to fix things before they broke, but Cian never listens. We can't go anywhere until it is fixed, but Cian doesn't have the right tools and he says he can't leave me on my own without protection. Looks like we're stuck here for a while!

F: We had some bread and leftover pigeon for breakfast then headed off at first light. Dad's chariot might be old, but he looks after it well. He keeps telling me I'll have my own chariot some day and I should fix things before they break. I just nodded and pretended to listen while he went on and on about it.

Then, as if to prove his point, we saw a chariot with a banjaxed wheel on up the road. Dad squinted the way he always does when he sees something suspicious, and stopped our chariot. He took his favourite spear, checked his sword and jumped out onto the road. I went to go after him but he told me to stay where I was. I never get to go anywhere!

D: Just our luck! The first person to come along looked like a bandit. Not that I've ever seen a bandit, but he looked like how I'd imagine one to look. A big burly man carrying a spear was walking towards us. I could only really make out his silhouette as the morning sun was behind him, but even his silhouette was scary.

Cian told me to wait in the chariot while he took his own spear and went down the road to meet him. Although he was trying to hide it, I knew Cian was a bit nervous. I don't blame him — I was too.

F: Dad and the young man talked for a while, then Dad came back. 'It's all right,' he said, 'just a brother and sister who need help fixing their wheel. I have some tools. You can go and talk to the sister if you want — we might be a while.' Dad always told me to help a stranger in need as it might be one of the gods in disguise. I went up to the girl who was covered in mud. She was a good bit older than me and sat on a chest by the side of the road. She smiled as I approached. I was all tongue-tied as I never know what to say to girls, but she was really nice to me.

D: While the big man helped Cian with the wheel, his son came over to talk to me. He looked a bit shy so I smiled at him and started talking. I had lots of little foster-brothers so I know what kind of things interest them. It turns out he's on his way to his new foster home. Awww — gods bless him — he looked so vulnerable sitting there. I remember how I felt when I first left home, so I told him not to worry and that he would be well looked after and learn loads of new things. It would be strange at first, but he'd soon get used to it, and before he knew it, he'd be heading back home.

F: Wow — it turns out the girl is on her way back home from being fostered and she loved it. I feel a lot better talking to someone who's been through it. She's really nice — I like her. We talked for ages. I told her about my family and my sister who'd been kidnapped. I said I could hardly remember her, but I remembered her doll with the straw hair and the checked dress.

D: When the little boy told me that his sister had been taken in a raid and was probably dead, I felt terrible for him. Then he told me about the doll she had. I stood up and opened the chest I was sitting on that had all my belongings inside it and showed him something.

F: By the gods and the gods of my ancestors!! I ran over to Dad, who thought I was busting for a pee as I was jumping up and down that much. He told me to find a tree and go against it. 'No, Dad, no! I don't need a pee! She – she – that girl is my sister Deirdre!' Dad didn't believe me until he went over and looked at her face.

D: The big man was my dad! I had no idea my poor family thought I was lost to them. I looked into the face of this man who was my father. And my little brother Ferdia, who was a toddler when I left, was grinning at me like a goose eating a cabbage. I had indeed been kidnapped in a raid, but my brave foster-father came and rescued me. He was killed by the raiders, but I managed to get away safely. A second messenger was sent to say I'd been found and all was well, but it seems Mum and Dad never got the message. Perhaps the messenger was himself killed by bandits — these are dangerous times.

F: I've never seen my father so happy. The four of us made our way back to Cian and Deirdre's settlement in the shadow of the great mound at Eamhain Mhacha. It is here where I am to spend the next ten years of my life, learning the ways of the warrior. Tomorrow, Dad will return home with Deirdre, and although I will not see them again for a long time, I am happy. Tonight we will feast with my new foster family and celebrate the return of a long-lost sister.

In the decade he spent with his foster family, Ferdia went on to learn all the skills he needed to become a warrior. Now grown up, he has his own chariot (which he looks after properly) and is soon to be married. He may be a fully-fledged warrior, but does his spear of honesty always fly true? **Answers below.**

A) A FEE ALWAYS HAS TO BE PAID TO THE FOSTERING FAMILY.

B) THE FEE FOR A GIRL IS HIGHER THAN FOR A BOY.

C) AFTER THEIR FOSTERAGE IS OVER, THE KIDS ARE EXPECTED TO LOOK AFTER THEIR FOSTER FAMILY IN DIFFICULT TIMES.

D) FOSTERED KIDS ARE GIVEN DIFFERENT FOODS ACCORDING TO THEIR RANK.

ANSWERS: Ferdia only lied once. a) Not always. Parents paid other tribes to foster their children so they could learn new skills and strengthen the bonds between tribes. But sometimes children were fostered out of affection. Close family, like aunts and uncles, might foster a child for that reason. b) True. The price was three 'sets' (one set was worth half the value of a milk cow) for the son of a chief and four sets for a daughter. c) Absolutely. The whole point of fosterage was to strengthen bonds. d) True. Stirabout (porridge) was given to all kids, but it was flavoured with salt butter for lower ranks, fresh butter for the kids of chieftains and honey for the children of kings.

ROUNDHOUSERS
A CELTIC SOAP OPERA

Over the centuries, loads of stuff from the Celtic era has been discovered in Ireland. Some of it was found in bogs, which preserved it, and some of it was buried treasure hoards. Other things were found in graves with their owners. Most of it ended up in museums. See if you can find these things in this episode of *Roundhousers*.

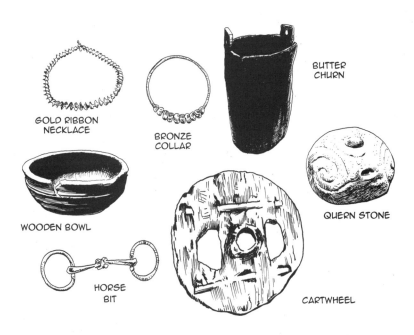

GOLD RIBBON
NECKLACE

BRONZE
COLLAR

BUTTER
CHURN

WOODEN BOWL

QUERN STONE

HORSE
BIT

CARTWHEEL

SCABBARD

SWORD HILT

TANKARD

FEASTING CUP

BRONZE DISC

BRONZE BOWL

BROOCH

128

129

130

131

132

133

134

135

DID YOU FIND ALL THE OBJECTS FROM THE MUSEUMS? ANSWERS ON PAGE 144.

NEXT TIME ON

Roundhousers

KING CONALL MESSES UP A CATTLE-RAID AND
GRÁINNE GETS A NEW FOSTER-BROTHER.

ÉIRES AND GRACES
LEGACY OF THE CELTS

Today, Ireland considers itself to be a Celtic nation, along with Scotland, the Isle of Man, Wales, Cornwall and Brittany, where Celtic culture has lasted. Celtic art can be seen all over Ireland with swirling patterns and intertwined knots decorating everything from stamps to coins to manhole covers.

There is a large statue of Cú Chulainn in the GPO in Dublin and other statues of the famous Celtic hero all over the country. And thanks to the monks who wrote the tales down in the early days of Christianity, the Celtic myths and legends have survived.

Also from early Christian Ireland, the beautiful Book of Kells and other illuminated manuscripts were illustrated in a breathtaking Celtic style, and many elaborately carved Celtic crosses still dot Ireland's landscape.

Modern Irish people have the Celtic appreciation of art, learning and stories, as well as the love of a good fight and the gift of the gab. Lots of names of regions, cities, towns and rivers in Ireland, Britain and Europe have a Celtic connection. The Irish language has words that are similar to others in other 'Celtic' languages. And we can see Celtic words in English too.

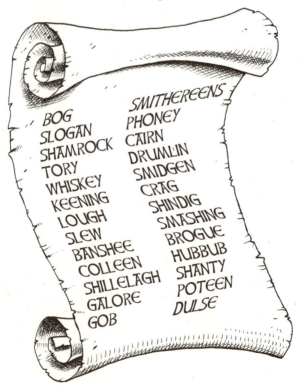

BOG
SLOGAN
SHAMROCK
TORY
WHISKEY
KEENING
LOUGH
SLEW
BANSHEE
COLLEEN
SHILLELAGH
GALORE
GOB

SMITHEREENS
PHONEY
CAIRN
DRUMLIN
SMIDGEN
CRAG
SHINDIG
SMASHING
BROGUE
HUBBUB
SHANTY
POTEEN
DULSE

Irish authors W.B. Yeats and Lady Gregory made Celtic folk tales popular in the early 20th century, and their books are still read everywhere. There are famous stage plays with a Celtic theme, such as John Millington Synge's *Deirdre of the Sorrows* and Brian Friel's *Dancing at Lughnasa*.

There are loads of football, rugby and basketball teams with 'Celtic' in their names, even as far away as America and South Africa. Popular music and dance have taken inspiration from Celtic myths and folklore, with singers, bands and dance groups enjoying international fame.

Many TV shows, films, games, books and comics feature Celtic-style heroes and characters. The famous King Arthur may well have been a Celt, and Merlin the magician a druid.

There are people the world over who swear they've heard the eerie cry of the banshee and others who say they've had encounters with faeries. Halloween, inspired by the Celtic festival of Samhain, now rivals Christmas in popularity. The modern wearing of scary costumes, going door to door collecting goodies, and lighting bonfires are all Celtic traditions.

Museums are filled with beautiful Celtic artefacts, and there are reconstructions of roundhouses and crannógs in Ireland, Britain and Europe, with actors playing the parts of Celtic people. These attract thousands of visitors every year, with no signs of interest in Celtic culture slowing down.

The Celts may not have left any great architecture behind, like the Greeks and Romans did. They may not have written much down, yet a Celtic legacy has continued well into the 21st century. That's pretty *DEADLY!* for a bunch of barbarians!

TIMELINE

700–600 BCE – Celts begin arriving in Ireland towards the end of the Bronze Age.

500 BCE – The Iron Age in Ireland begins.

390–200 BCE – The Clonycavan man is sacrificed around this time. His body is found preserved in a bog early in the 21st Century.

200 BCE – Carvings on the Turoe Stone, Co. Galway, show European La Tène influence.

100 BCE – The Celts build a series of roads called slite throughout Ireland.

95 BCE – A great temple is built – and destroyed – at Eamhain Mhacha.

43 BCE – Pomponius Mela writes about how Ireland is rich with grassland and exploding cattle.

35 BCE – Diodorus Siculus writes in his Historical Library that the Irish eat human flesh. Was he fibbing or was Ireland full of ZOMBIES?!

AD 82 – Roman general Gnaeus Julius Agricola considers conquering Ireland but returns to Rome where he dies of food poisoning.

AD 140 – Greek map-maker Claudius Ptolemy makes the first known map of Ireland.

AD 400 – Niall Noigiallach (Niall of the Nine Hostages) rules Ireland.

AD 403 – A 16-year-old boy named Maewyn Succat is kidnapped by Irish raiders from his home in Britain and sold into slavery. He later escapes, becomes a bishop and calls himself Patrick.

AD 432 – Saint Patrick arrives, bringing Christianity to Ireland. The Celtic age ends.

All dates are approximate.

ANSWERS TO INSIDE A ROUNDHOUSE

1) Goat and sheepskins
2) Cauldrons
3) Fidchell board game
4) Leather tanning frame
5) Child minding the fire
6) Slave gathering dung for manure and daub
7) Goose guard 'dog'
8) Animal pens
9) Oven
10) Quern
11) Butter churn

ANSWERS TO ROUNDHOUSERS

GOLD RIBBON
NECKLACE
PAGE 129

BRONZE
COLLAR
PAGE 129

WOODEN
BOWL
PAGE 129

BUTTER CHURN
PAGE 129

QUERN
STONE
PAGE 130

HORSE
BIT
PAGE
131

CARTWHEEL
PAGE 131

SWORD HILT
& SCABBARD
PAGE 132

BROOCH
PAGE 133

FEASTING CUP & TANKARD
PAGE 133

BRONZE DISC
PAGE 133

BRONZE BOWL
PAGE 135